Book Design: B Martin Pedersen, Lauren Slutsky

Total Sports Publishing website: www.totalsportspublishing.com

*I'd like to thank
the following
people and organi-
zations for their
role in shaping my
career over the
years: Mike
Ehret, an old
friend and
the model athlete
in my earliest
pictures, taken in
East Orange.
Sports Illustrated
for such a
wonderful forty
years, and Steve
Fine, its director
of photography,
for the best years
in my career.
Steve Sabol and
NFL Films, for
their inspirational
footage. Neil
Leifer, a great
photographer
and my former
arch-rival, who
was a driving
force in my career.
My parents,
grandfather, wife
Eva, and sons
Christian and
Bjorn for their
love and support.
To all the players
who have
sacrificed their
bodies and
mortgaged their
futures for the
love of the game.
Finally, to the few
PR people who
spelled my name
correctly on my
field passes over
the years,
eliminating the
horror of trying to
pick up a field
pass for Misters
Toos, Josse, Iosst,
Yoce, and dozens
of other
abominations —
my two personal
favorites being
Slater Looss and
Mr. Walter Loass.
It's a great world.*

GLADIATORS

40 YEARS OF FOOTBALL
PHOTOGRAPHS BY WALTER IOOSS

COMMENTARY BY ROY BLOUNT, JR.

KINGSTON, NEW YORK NEW YORK, NEW YORK

"You see the pigskin way up high, you feel the clench in your thigh. You fight to win, You guys, Oh how cruel." "Football" by an 11 yr. old.

For Sports Illustrated Magazine.   December 13, 1962. Yankee Stadium. The Bronx. Pittsburgh

. You do it any way you choose. Beware the big guys, all tall and full. Smash the small

New York Giants. Andy Robustelli #81 and Theron Sapp #33.

The love affair started on December 28, 1958 in East Orange, N.J. I was 15. I was with my father and grandfather on the third floor of our house, listening to the Colts vs. Giants "sudden death" championship game on the radio. The game that put pro football on the map, and is often called "The greatest game ever played."

The Colts won the game and my heart.

This is not a story of boy meets girl, but of boy meets football, photography, and especially the Baltimore Colts' Johnny Unitas and Raymond Berry. It was Berry's number, 82, that I always wore on my football jersey. He was slow and had good hands: just like me. I started cutting pages out of *Sport* magazine and *Sports Illustrated* and hanging them along all four walls of an empty room in our house. During high-school classes I drew football players—the form of their bodies in motion.

In the spring of '59 my father, a professional jazz bassist, resumed an old hobby of his, photography. He bought an Asahi Pentax 35mm camera, a 135mm and a 300mm lens, and two New York Giants season tickets. Back then NFL teams played six home games a season, and the Giants' home field was Yankee Stadium. My father would bring his gear and shoot from his seat. I showed no interest in his hobby until the next-to-the-last game. I shot part of a roll. I found a special pleasure in viewing life through a telephoto lens, editing out the unnecessary. I don't remember much about that game, but my memory of processing the film back in East Orange is still vivid. Holding the wet roll up to the light and seeing the images. They danced in my head. I was hooked.

To practice my new hobby I arranged games to be played amongst my friends, who were equally obsessed with sports, at a field near our high school. We would all wear our football jerseys, we would tape up our hands and socks and shoes to look good, and we emphasized the passing game. I would be Raymond Berry for awhile, then I would take pictures of the other guys for awhile. All my friends wanted to see how fantastic they looked. This is where I began to follow focus with a 300mm lens: focusing by hand on the move. At the time this was an absolute necessity to make it in the business. Now, after so many years working with auto-focus lenses, I've lost the knack. It's like safe-cracking: if you don't use that touch, you lose it.

My father and I would also shoot from the stands at other sporting events—basketball at Madison Square Garden, baseball at Yankee Stadium and Connie Mack Stadium in Philly. By now I was in love with sports photography.

In the summer of 1960, to get some basic photographic knowledge, I took a six-week accelerated course at the Germain School of Photography in lower Manhattan. Every morning I took the Lackawanna Railroad in from East Or-

ange. If any one thing summed up my new-found devotion to photography it was this: I had to give up my beloved stickball, a game I had played all day, every day, until dark or until my pitching arm was so sore I couldn't lift it to eat. Now every evening I walked back from the train station by way of our stickball field, to find out how many home runs each of my friends had hit that day (we always kept our stats), how far I had fallen behind in the home run race.

That course was my total formal education in photography, but it helped get me ready for experience, which I jumped into early. That fall a friend of my grandfather's who had graduated from Princeton put me in touch with the college's P.R. man, who issued me a sideline credential for a game against Columbia in return for prints of my shots. I was building my portfolio.

In the spring of '61 I called George Bloodgood, assistant picture editor at *Sports Illustrated*. I told him I would like to meet him and show him my portfolio. He no doubt realized from my tone of voice that I was young and nervous. I'll never forget what he asked: "You got any nudes in your portfolio?" "Nudes?" I stammered. He told me to come to his office at the Time & Life Building on Sixth Avenue in Manhattan.

Bloodgood started giving me "spec" assignments. I would shoot a particular player, *SI* would process the film, and Bloodgood would critique what I'd done. It was beyond my friends' comprehension—I was getting a hundred dollars a day to get on the sidelines of a football game. A lot of people weren't making a hundred bucks a week working full-time. In May of '61, when I was still a senior at East Orange High School, I got my first full-fledged assignment. Back then *SI* had a one-page feature called "Pat on the Back." I was sent to Groton, Connecticut, to shoot octogenarian sailor Archie Chester, who had built his own sailboat. I had three cameras wrapped around my neck, I was rowing a little boat so I could shoot Archie in his boat—I was so nervous I got seasick on water that was flat as a pancake. They used my picture. It covered three fourths of the page. I still have a picture of Archie and me, that my father took. My father went with me on the assignment.

By 1962 I was doing jobs for both *Sports Illustrated* and *Sport*. But that fall something special happened. I took my first trip to Baltimore—to Mecca, by train—and I had a sideline credential for the Colts. I wore all khaki-colored clothes. I might be seen on my favorite show, Thursday

My first Photo
November 1959, Yankee Stadium, The Bronx, New York, NY Giants vs. Chicago Cardinals

My house - East Orange, New Jersey - February 1959

Walter Iooss & Jim Drake, 1968 Olympics, Mexico City

night pro football highlights. Since the show was in black and white, I figured the light color of khaki would show up better on TV, if by some chance I got on.

With the Colts trailing and less than two minutes to play, Unitas threw to Jimmy Orr near the end zone. Orr juggled the ball, held on, and scored the game-winning touchdown. This happened right in front of me. I took one shot with my 180mm lens and then ran onto the field and jumped onto Orr's back, patting him on the shoulder pads, like the deranged Colt fan I was. A photographer's not supposed to do that.

On the train ride home I was elated about the Colts' win, but despondent that I might have missed the shot of Orr. I processed the film later that night and was amazed that my one shot of the catch was tack sharp and near perfect. My first great action shot. (See page 98.) That night I was featured on Pro Football highlights, deliriously pounding on poor Jimmy Orr. I probably weighed twenty pounds more than he did back then. It was such a wonderful catch, they replay it a lot, and I'm part of the catch. The tape always ends the moment I stop patting Orr's back. When ESPN did an hour special on my football photography they showed the catch, and they interviewed Orr. He remembered the catch. He didn't remember me, of course.

Football has changed enormously since 1962. So much of the grit of the game has been removed. Better field drainage and less use of baseball fields for football have eliminated the mud that was so photogenic. Some of the

East Orange, New Jersey - January 1960

East Orange, New Jersey - October 1961

best uniforms and helmets have been replaced—for instance the Eagles' kelly-green uniforms and helmets. Domes have replaced the old intimate stadiums that had wonderful backgrounds. Even the way the fans look has been altered by officially licensed NFL clothing. Fans used to wear their everyday work clothes to a game. Now they look like out-of-shape players in their jerseys. Four-o'clock starts have taken away the good light. (In September, in some stadiums, the light at that time is wonderful, but in winter the sun has dropped behind the stadium and there's no real daylight at all.) Artificial turf and indoor arenas have destroyed the mood on the field. Some facemasks hide the player's face and expressions. Herds of media and too many commercials have broken the flow of the game. The Super Bowl, which should be the climax of the season, is usually the season's worst game. And what is it with all the indoor skyrockets at the Super Bowl? Football used to supply the fireworks. I guess I am getting old.

I still love the game that an editorial in the New York Times once called "the most violent team sport yet created by man," but I miss so much of the soul that has vanished into those corporate Skyboxes. No doubt the photos I've taken in the '90s will look like the good old days 20 years from now, but these days I miss the '60s and '70s. Johnny U., Raymond, Memorial Stadium…. I wish I could go back in time and take the perfect picture I never took of John Unitas. It still bothers me that the greatest shot of Unitas is not by me. Same with Jim Brown. The legends. I got some good ones of them, though.

East Orange, New Jersey, circa 1960

Los Angeles Rams vs San Diego Chargers, Coliseum, Los Angeles, California, October 1979.

"Football," the great Deacon Jones once intoned, "is a combination of accepting pain, tolerating pain, applying pain. I love it because I come from the ghetto, it was natural for me. I had a lot of hostilities in my heart and soul because of circumstances that I was raised on…. Had I went into baseball I still would have maintained all those hostilities inside me. Football allowed me the pleasure of releasing those hostilities, 'cause I had a chance to go down there in the pit and hit something, and the harder I hit, the more I released those hostilities."

Yes. Yes. And we wouldn't have it any other way, we who witness the hitting (and release our own poor piddling hostilities) from a safe distance. But that distance also lends an enchantment that transcends the pit. The World Wrestling Federation's football league will no doubt produce pain-talk that will make the Deacon sound like a deacon. The great thing about *real* football, violence *sort of* aside, is how much it pleases the eye.

Where else will you get to see 22 enormous men jammed together in a frieze, straining with all their might along an imaginary line? Again, at the one-foot line. And again, at the one-inch line. And then, maybe, or maybe not, spilling into the end zone like clowns from an undersized car.

Where else are you going to see a 200-plus-pound man hit in such a way that he hangs upside down in thin air over hard ground, and when he lands on his head he will shake it off, like the roadrunner in the cartoons, and rise to be flipped again?

Where else are you going to see an outfit of hat, pads, knickers, jersey and cleats that is so otherworldly, when you think about it, and yet so cool?

And the numbers! The largest, most vivid numerals you will ever see a human being wear on his body. Football-jersey numbers are identity and also a target—the ideal place to hit someone with a pass or a hand-off, or with hostility.

Where else are you going to see hostility delivered, and evaded, with such torque and grace?

If all this sounds too aesthetic to you, sitting there on the couch, with your beer and your chips, worrying for the umpteenth time about the points, let Walter Iooss show you what football looks like to someone who is always seeing it fresh.

Maybe the way you saw it when you were a kid.

Think back. Here's probably the first thing you noticed: Balls are supposed to be round. What's with this one?

"That's a football," an elder tells you, so you give it a kick. It bobbles around oddly. You pick it up, as best you can. Good to the touch. Before long you are running with it (it's the only ball you run with, unless you count rugby), and somebody is chasing you, making you squeal not in pain but with delight. And as you get older your frame of reference expands, and you begin to dream that you're a pro. Destined to be an immortal.

A baseball is round. You whip it around the infield, you run around the bases. A basketball is round, there are round lines on the floor, you have shoot-arounds, you move the ball around and put it in a round hole. In golf, again, the round hole, and you play a round. Tennis, ping-pong,

bocce, bowling, cricket, croquet…. Even in soccer, which is what most of the world calls football, the ball, like the earth, is a sphere. But in American football, the ball is shaped like…

What? A shoe? A pod? A symmetrical egg, layable in either direction? Two snubbed nosecones joined back to back? At any rate it has a blunt point at each end. It is a ball with a pronounced, ever-reversible linear dimension. Gradually you come to realize it is designed to be shoved as directly as possible down the other team's throat.

It is also designed to be held. Feels good to the hand, like your dog's head or the nape of your sweetie's neck. A basketball has a similar texture, but unless you can palm it, a basketball is always just at or off your fingertips, it doesn't tuck under your arm like… a baby? When you grip a football, you get possessive. A football has that nice pebble grain and also seams and also laces. A baseball has seams (one seam, really, and yet we speak of a two-seam or a four-seam fastball), so it involves interesting tactile orientation, but the only time you really possess a baseball without needing to throw it again, it's in your glove. And hey, I love the feel of a baseball as much as you do, but basically it's a rock. Nobody says, "He can really throw the baseball." People do say, "He can really throw the football."

And you want to throw the football, and kick it, in neither case a simple matter. Other balls naturally rotate, bounce straight, roll predictably. The only reason you impart a funny spin to a round ball is to make it go, or bounce, crooked. You have to put action on a football to make it go straight. We speak of a perfect spiral, but it is never quite perfect, as we can see in closeups of a long forward pass: there is always a bit of a wobble at the nose, as if the ball is a dog sniffing out a trail. Essentially, though, the course of a punt or a pass is a helix, like a strand of DNA. A place kick, on the other hand (though not so pronouncedly as in the old pre-soccer-style days), is end-over-end. A football bounce is a bit of both—you never know how it's going to go. It may leap crazily up off the ground like a fish out of water, or it may go bonky-wonky-bonky in roughly the direction you hope for, or in the direction you dread, or back and forth—loose ball!—away from everybody. Football is the only game measured, constantly, in yards or fractions of yards—the most directional of games, played with the least directional of balls.

So when your team has the ball, it is lined up perpendicular to the linear goal, but you know it's not going to go like an arrow because of the way it is built—a bulbous, treacherous arrow. And also because of the way the people in your way are built—bulbous, desperate men.

But we're getting ahead of ourselves. When you first play football (unless you've just been imported from Tonga or Lithuania to ride through college on your instep), it's against other kids. Aside from falling off your bike or out of your treehouse, the first serious full-body jolt you are likely to receive in America is in pickup football. At recess and in the street you play touch, but you can still get your block knocked off by a block. This, at least to coaches, is the most important aspect of football: hitting. You go out for the high-school team and find yourself engaged, whump, bump, in endless, grinding contact drills. In baseball you hit the ball, in basketball you hit baskets, but in organized football you hit each other.

You may decide at this point to stick with disorganized touch, in which everybody has a chance to dream that he's a pro. If you are determined to get with the program, your coaches yell at you to go hard and to master the fundamental techniques of hitting, and one day you deliver your momentum into somebody larger than yourself, just so, and knock him flat. And you hardly feel it yourself; it's kind of dreamy. One of the few pure pleasures of adolescence.

In other ball games, you are generally not supposed to run full-tilt into an opponent. On every play in American football, that is what most of the players hunger for: a shot at putting another guy on his back. Even the guy whose job is to throw, catch or carry has to have a taste for, or at least a willingness to accept, collision. If you carry enough momentum of your own into the crunch, you are less likely— somewhat less likely—to be injured. It as if you fall off a building, and as you are plummeting toward the pavement you bear in mind that if you can manage to fall harder it will be better. This usually does not apply to the quarterback. As he is falling off the building he has to bear in mind the patterns his receivers are running, and the ways the defense is trying to foil those patterns, and all the different directions that the pavement may be coming from, and moves he can make to avoid the pavement without shirking his job. But generally speaking, if you don't knock them down, they will you.

You can develop an appetite for that. Especially if you get your face skinned up cosmetically, for the next day at school. Maybe you've got a little limp. A cast, even. Cool. And on Friday night, under lights, cheerleaders! They just call you Mr. Touchdown. Or, more likely, they call somebody else that: a member of your peer group who makes you realize that some people are born with more hero-potential than others. But even if you are just barely good enough to compete at the high-school level, you can summon up more grit than you knew was in you, and you can wear a letter jacket, and you can give it to a majorette, your majorette, to wear around school. Very few guys are ever going to date models or starlets, but you never forget your majorette. Nor do you forget the other guys with whom you get sweaty, sore and jocular.

In high school, already, you may blow out your knee. Or, more likely, you come to realize that you are too slow or too small, or both, to play in college. From now on you are a fan, and you play some touch: back to dreaming—in a smaller part of your mind, now—that you are a pro. If you are good enough to play in college, you find that you are already a pro, sort of.

The potential for glory is greater than in high school, but so is the grind and the ambivalence. Your coaches own you. The National Collegiate Athletic Association won't let you make money, for yourself: just for your place of higher learning and for the NCAA. It's hard, trying to study for an Intro to Philosophy exam after four hours of butting heads

and getting your blocking assignments down, and unless you are smarter than most people your size, you have to cut corners with the books. People help you cut them.

You cheat, and are cheated. But you're playing serious ball, with and against guys who are not only amazing but famous. You get to be stronger and more adept than you thought you'd ever have to be, but relative to these amazing guys you are not as great as you thought you were. You line up across from some guy who eats your lunch, and you know there are probably guys who can eat his. You may blow out your knee. More likely, you come to realize that you are too slow or too small, or both, to go on to the next level.

But maybe you grew up in the streets or out in the sticks and you are dead set not to go back, and maybe you have some psychological issues that you can work through by your taste for what they call smash-mouth football, and you lift weights and do whatever else it takes to build a body that is useful for the one purpose of advancing that funky ball downfield or pushing it back. Your feet are quick enough, your instincts sharp enough, your perceptions clever enough, that you can summon your 200-pounds-plus-plus-plus and deliver. In college, too, there are cheerleaders. And alumni: paunchy grown men who look at you with shiny vicarious eyes and set you up in things. Maybe you even scare your coaches a little bit.

And against all the odds you get to be a pro. And probably everybody is just as quick, sharp, clever and bulky as you are, or more so. Say you're a running back. In college you found big holes and blew through them like the wind. In the pros, you take one step and that hole has narrowed to where you can maybe just slash through it. And then, maybe, sometimes, the American dream: open territory ahead. But the people you line up against are huge and highly combustible. A good many of them weigh 300-plus-plus-plus, and nimble withal. Steam is rising off of them. They are playing with broken fingers and torn abdominal muscles that won't start healing until the season's over, and with chipped vertebrae and swollen toes that will never stop hurting for the rest of their lives. They wish you ill. And even your teammates eschew supportive rah-rah. When Ricky Williams left the University of Texas to become a professional ballcarrier for the Saints, he missed the chummy sentiments of college, where his linemen "were so proud. When they missed a block and I got hit in the backfield, they would be right there and say, 'I'm sorry, Ricky.' You could see in their eyes that it really hurt them. In New Orleans when I got hit in the backfield, they'd pick me up but I never once heard anyone say, 'I'll get them next time,' or anything at all." When you pass from youth to adulthood in football it is as if somebody has said, "Square-dancing is fun with boys and girls. Let's see what it's like with bears." And they are growling all around you.

After the game these bears don't have campuses to lounge around on, they have families to deal with, maybe parole officers. Hangers-on love to help them run through their money. And as far as football goes, there is no higher level to dream toward; you have had your last graduation; this is it, and the next step is grim: ordinary life. Rocky Bleier, the old Steeler running back who managed to serve with distinction in the National Football League after being riddled with shrapnel and having part of his foot blown off in Vietnam, suggested to me once that football was psychologically harder than combat. In combat, you were fighting for your life, and taking cover. In football, you had to "show that you don't care about your body," as Bleier put it, so that they will let you keep putting yourself in harm's way. If you got injured badly enough in combat, your soldiering career was over. If you got injured badly enough in football, your football career was over. A disablement in combat is a reprieve. In football, it's a little death. You can't be a knight in shining armor anymore. With luck you can be a TV guy or a motivational speaker. The motivation of a pro football player is as complicated as the axes of the ball: a spiral of relish and dread, or a crazy bounce, or end over end. "It's not fun," said Bleier. "You could do something that would cause you to be put down or traded, or released outright." Like gladiators in the Colosseum or can-can dancers at the Moulin Rouge, pro football players are working, pushing through their pain to stay one step ahead of time's winged chariot, and there is something awful about the looks on their faces.

Awful, and yet ecstatic. It's an out-of-body experience, to dance with bears. Bears at whom many thousands of people are roaring. "Ever been cheered?" Joe Namath asked someone once. "Ever heard 60,000 people chant your name? It's indescribable, man." Photographable, though, by Iooss.

Say you're up in the stands yelling, waving a banner, caught up in the dream. Your team's linemen and the enemy's stand for a moment facing each other. They look like housing projects on each side of a narrow street, with laundry out. Then they get down, their noses almost touching. There is no no-man's-land to speak of. Crunch. Whang. Bang. And little guys (the ones in the 200-plus range) are running for their lives.

All of which, if you're a coach, can be—should be—reducible to x's and o's. Coaches dream on blackboards. Let's put it this way: NFL coaches don't like Doug Flutie. If you're a coach, in fact, you can't help bearing a certain animosity toward whoever your quarterback is. This cocky youngster is like someone dating your daughter: you don't trust him, and you don't really want him to have a good time. But there he goes off with the girl in his fast car. As for your kicker…. Well, everybody resents the kicker. This little world-music guy who hardly ever gets bumped, even, and whose little foot so often holds the game in its balance. And defensive backs hate receivers. Receivers get the ball thrown *to* them. And if they manage to catch it, they have beaten a defensive back. Defensive backs do all they can to take the pleasure out of the game for receivers. But if you're a coach you can't help feeling some resentment toward all your players: you don't want your fleet-footed giants to get away with what they yearn to get away with—improvising, lateralling off, venting their spleens, blitzing on instinct. You want them to work within your system.

Imagine a system constraining Mean Joe Greene or John Elway. But a pro football team is the largest and most technically enhanced and configured aggregation in sports. No one can grab the ball like Michael Jordan or Pedro Martinez and singlehandedly dominate the game.

However, football is like war: the generals can strategize all they want, but it comes down to mano-a-mano. And a great player does outshine not only the other guys but also the system. A rare great player is so good, and stays healthy and determined for so many years, and has the luck to play in so many unforgettable games, that he gets to be what you expected, when you were seven, to become in due time: a legend.

A legend stands atop an enormous pile of guys who peaked in the seventh grade or senior year of high school or senior year of college or before that third knee operation. He peaked at the top of the heap, and he held his king-of-the-mountain ground for season after season, so that when he retires he is up there for good. Personally, I find it hard to believe that anybody else is going to climb that heap. For one thing, today's overdeveloped players generate so many foot-pounds of pressure that they tend to deconstruct each other and themselves. For another thing, I hate to admit that anybody today is ever going to be as legendary as Jim Brown or Johnny Unitas or Paul Hornung or Joe Montana or Dick Butkus or Walter Payton or…okay, let a coach in: Vince Lombardi. Legends need to be at least nearly as old as I am.

At any rate, by the time a football guy is assured of immortality, he is approaching the twilight of his career, the autumn of his falls. Pretty soon he, like a fan, is a pro in his dreams.

Check out Iooss, though: fiftysomething years old, still taking snaps. He may get misty for the old days of iron men, wooden ships and muddy uniforms, but his eye cuts through the mist. Like a great linebacker he senses pressure—the swell and the undertow of the play—and responds. Like a great receiver he gets to the moment and has the eye and hands to catch it. If football photography were coach-directed, the coach would not like Iooss. He is legendary among his peers for calmly going against the pack, taking strange chances, setting up at unaccountable positions, and getting nothing but the game's one key picture. I remember watching Terry Bradshaw throw deep for John Stallworth in the Super Bowl and Stallworth was sprinting stride for stride with the defender and you could see Stallworth adjusting at full speeed to the flight of the ball behind him and I thought, "I know Stallworth will get it"—and Stallworth, a pro, twisted his body in the air in a dreamlike way and got it; and I thought "I know Iooss got it too." And there it was three days later on the cover of *Sports Illustrated.* Stallworth is in retirement now, but Walter is still catching dreams.

Whether Coast-to-Coast Iooss is still as much fun to travel with, I don't know. I know I'm not. I remember one time in Chicago, he and I and this legend….

But you are probably already looking at the pictures. I know I am.

Kids playing football, What Cheer, Iowa, October 1974

THEDREAM

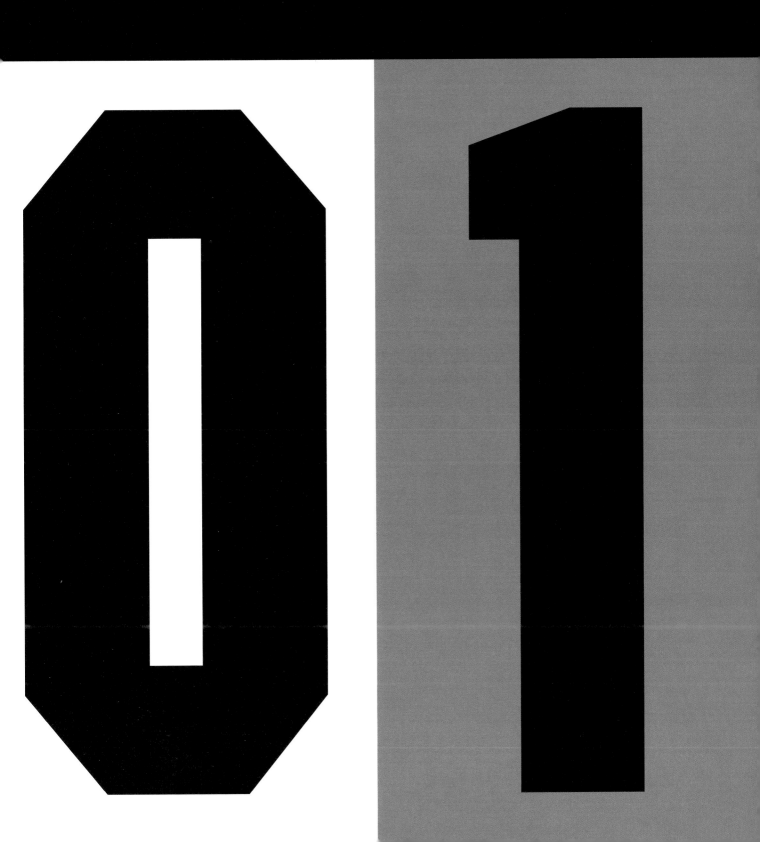

01

West Berlin, Vermont, October 1974

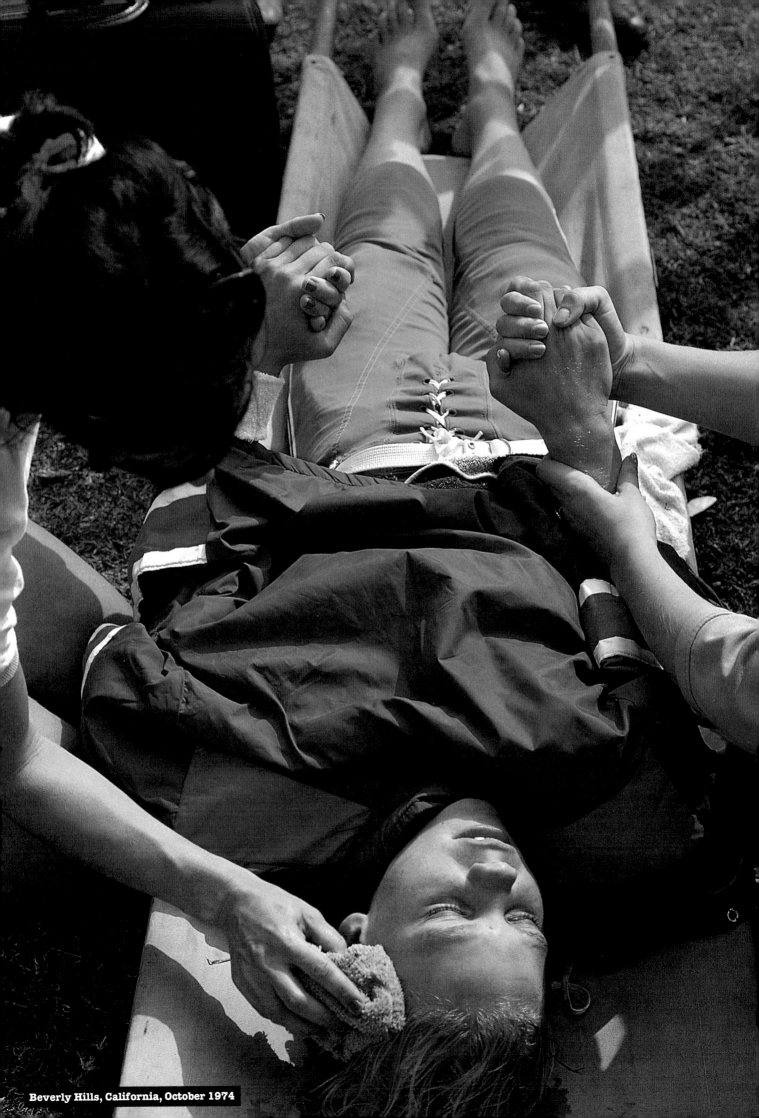

Beverly Hills, California, October 1974

Los Angeles, California, November 1974

Winter Park, Florida, November 1987

Taos, New Mexico, December 1974

COLLEGE

02

Bear Bryant, Tuscaloosa, Alabama, November 1981

Notre Dame vs Michigan, Ann Arbor, Michigan, September 1979

Army-Navy Game, Philadelphia, Pennsylvania, December 1980

Texas University fan outside a 7-11 store, Austin, Texas, November 1977

George Webster, Michigan State vs Ohio State, East Lansing, Michigan, October 1965

Donny Anderson, Texas Tech vs Baylor, Lubbock, Texas, October 1965

Michigan State player, East Lansing, Michigan, October 1965

Anthony Davis, U.S.C. vs Georgia Tech, Athens, Georgia, September 1973

Bear Bryant, Tuscaloosa, Alabama, October 1981

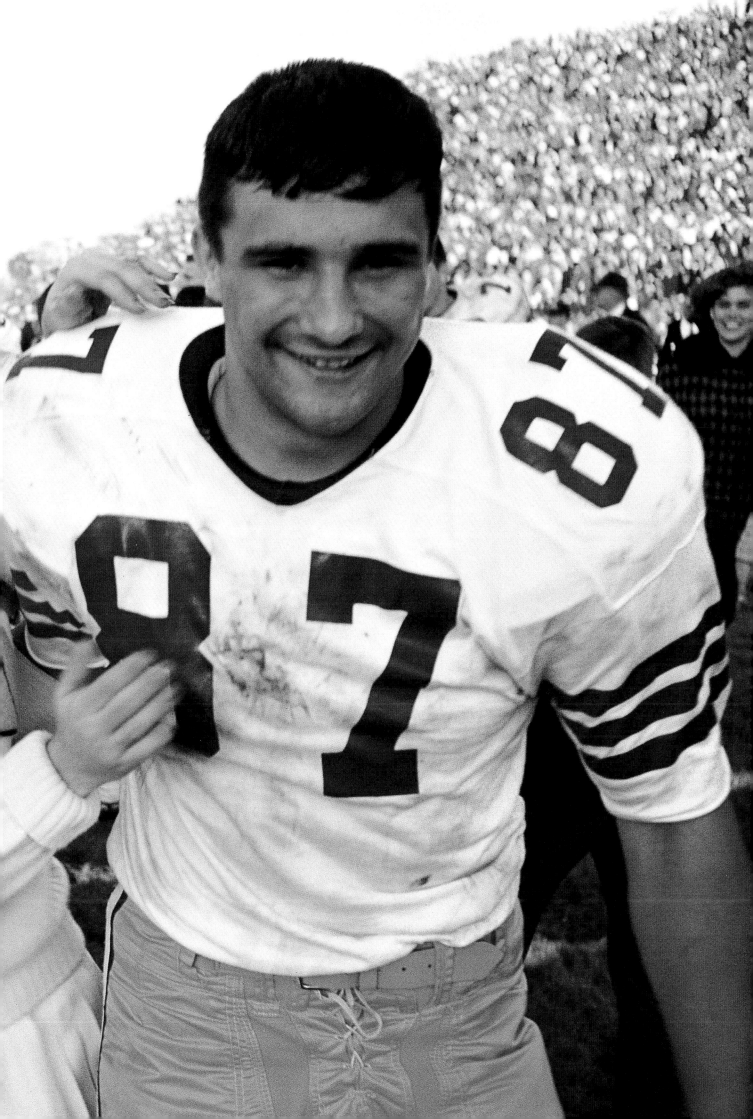

THE GAME

03

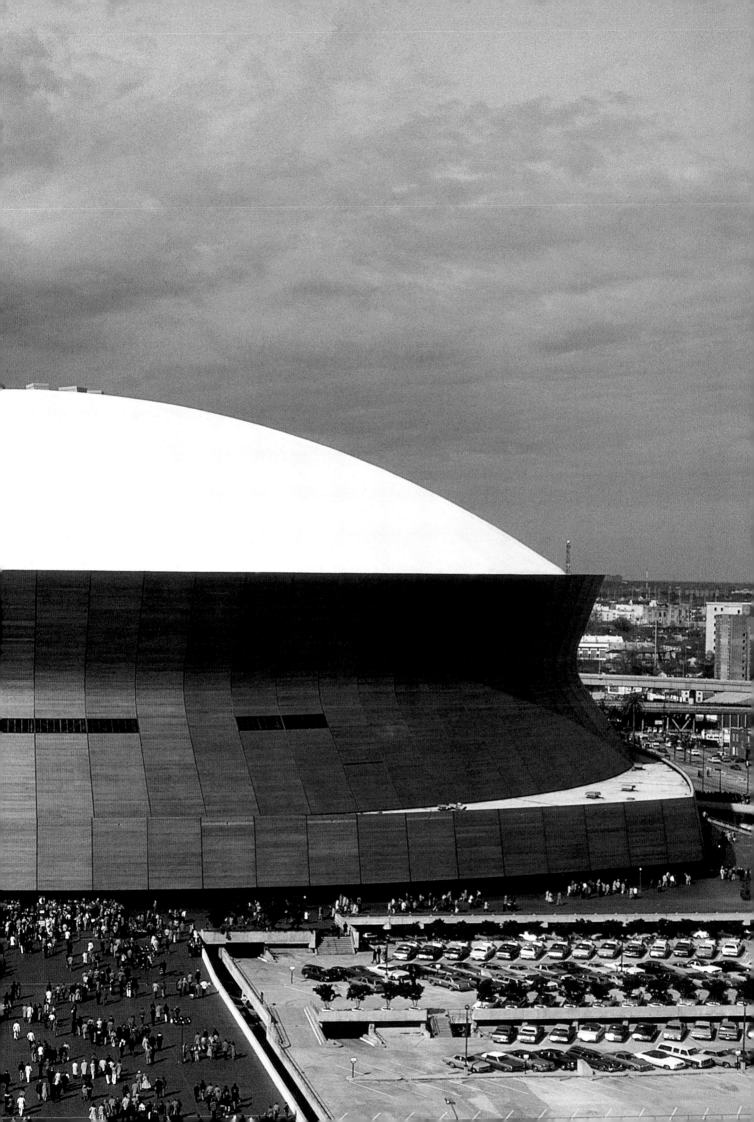

Dick Modzelewski, Cleveland Browns vs Green Bay Packers, Green Bay, Wisconsin, January 1966

Mark Van Eegan, Oakland Raiders vs Baltimore Colts, Baltimore, Maryland, January 1978

Jimmy Orr, Baltimore Colts vs San Francisco 49ers, Memorial Stadium, Baltimore, Maryland, October 1962

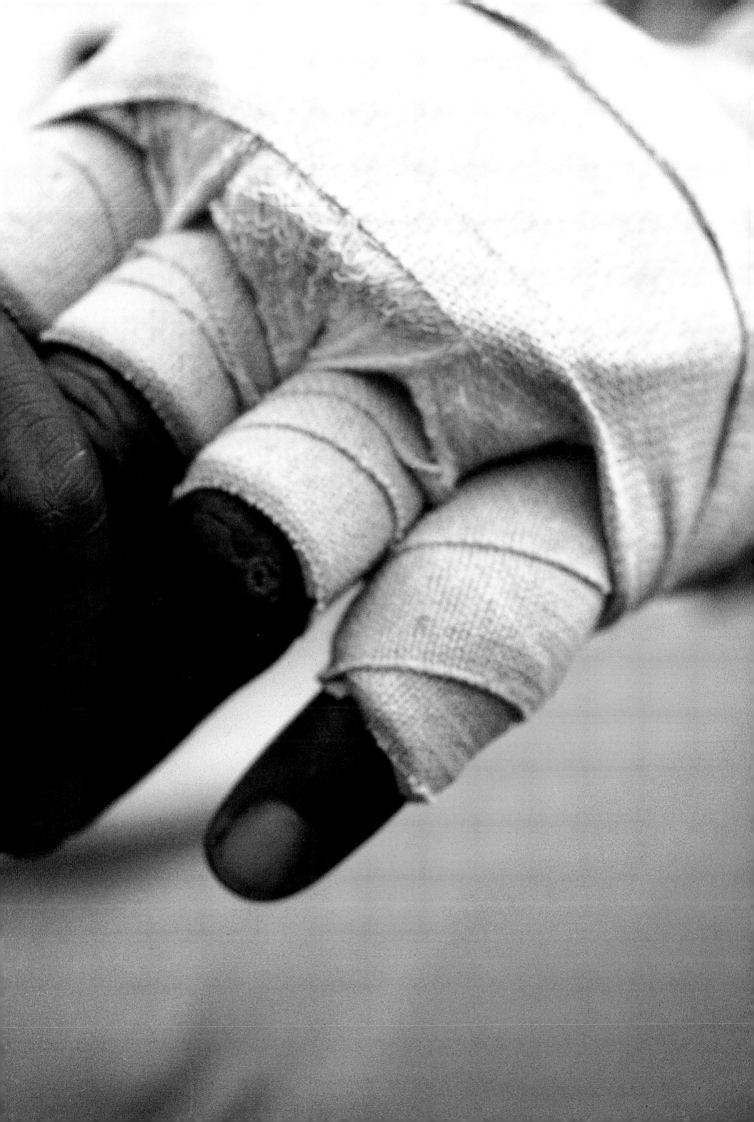

Calvin Hill, Dallas Cowboys vs Washington Redskins, Washington, D.C., October 1973

Jon Kolb, Pittsburgh Steelers at Oakland Coliseum, Oakland, California, December 1973

Roger Staubach, Dallas Cowboys vs Atlanta Falcons, Texas Stadium, Irving, Texas, December 1978

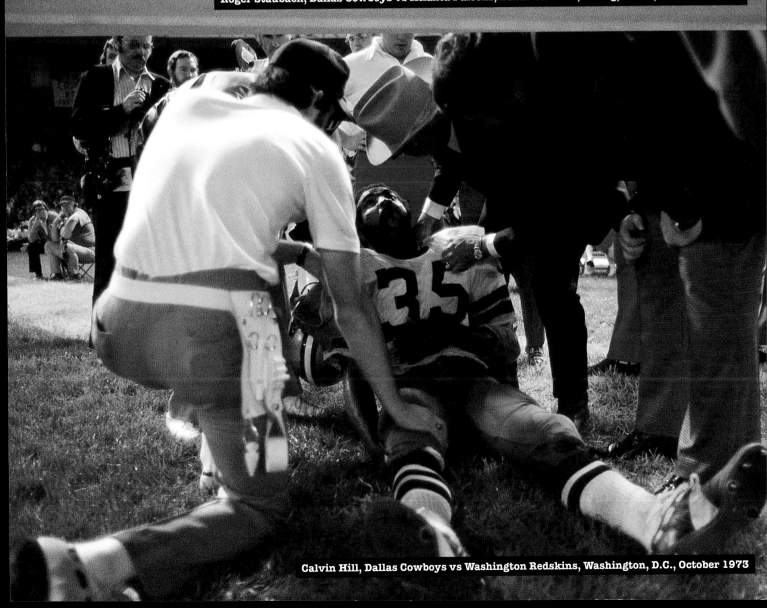

Calvin Hill, Dallas Cowboys vs Washington Redskins, Washington, D.C., October 1973

Jon Kolb, Pittsburgh Steelers, Three Rivers Stadium, Pittsburgh, Pennsylvania, October 1979

Roger Staubach, Dallas Cowboys vs Washington Redskins, R.F.K. Memorial Stadium, Washington, D.C., November 1972

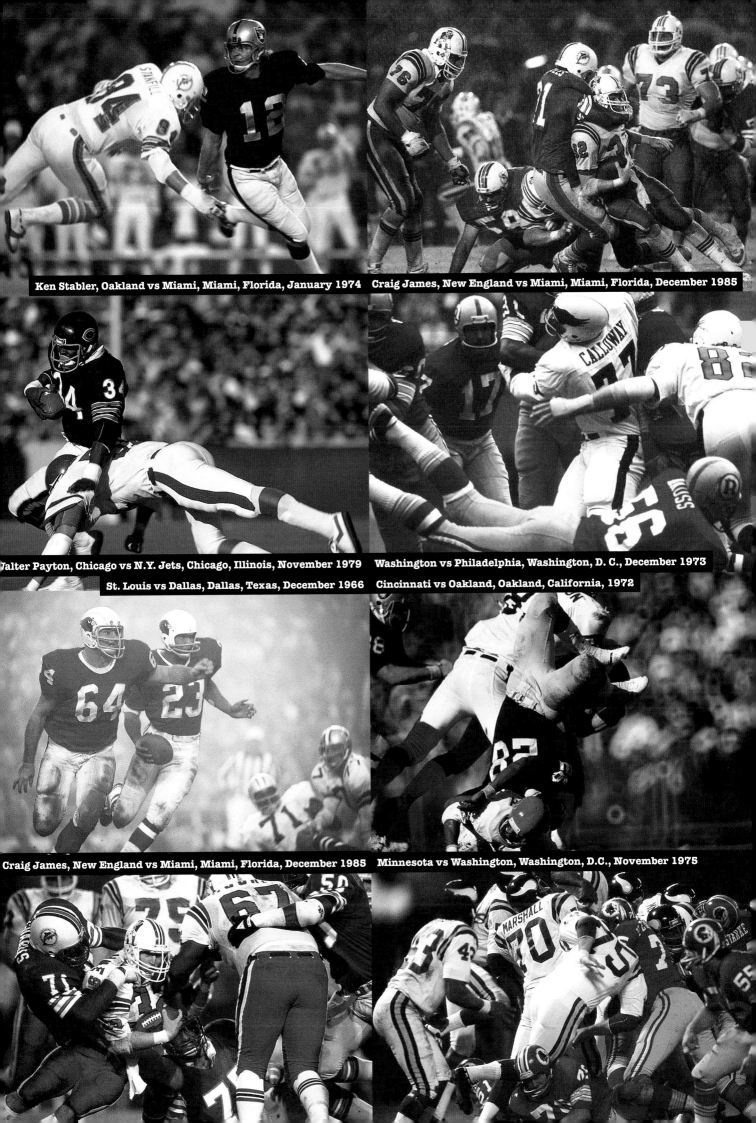

Ken Stabler, Oakland vs Miami, Miami, Florida, January 1974

Craig James, New England vs Miami, Miami, Florida, December 1985

Walter Payton, Chicago vs N.Y. Jets, Chicago, Illinois, November 1979

Washington vs Philadelphia, Washington, D. C., December 1973

St. Louis vs Dallas, Dallas, Texas, December 1966

Cincinnati vs Oakland, Oakland, California, 1972

Craig James, New England vs Miami, Miami, Florida, December 1985

Minnesota vs Washington, Washington, D.C., November 1975

Riverfront Stadium, Cincinnati, Ohio, Pittsburgh Steelers vs Cincinnati Bengals, December 1976

Steelers Fans, Three Rivers Stadium, Pittsburgh, Pennsylvania, October 1973

Super Bowl Fan, Halftime Show, Tulane Stadium, New Orleans, Louisiana, January 1970

Raiders Fan, Memorial Stadium, Baltimore, Maryland, December 1970

Exotic Dancer, Super Bowl IX, Pittsburgh vs Minnesota, January 1975

National Anthem, Tampa Bay Bucs, The Sombrero, Tampa, Florida, November 1979

Peeping Pedro, Los Angeles Coliseum, Los Angeles, California, October 1980

Orange Bowl, Miami Dolphins Game, Miami, Florida, October 1985

WOMEN WOMEN WOMEN WOMEN WOMEN

REST ROOMS

Cowboy Fan, Texas Stadium, Irving, Texas, October 1981

Fans, Tampa Stadium, Tampa, Florida, November 1979

Oakland Raiders Rookie, Oakland Raiders Training Camp, Santa Rosa, California, July 1984

Linesmen, Super Bowl XXII at Jack Murphy Stadium, San Diego, California, January 1988

Field Goal, San Francisco 49ers vs Tampa Bay Bucs, San Francisco, California, October 1994

Cleveland Browns, Municipal Stadium, Cleveland, Ohio, October 1979

Emmitt Smith, Dallas Cowboys vs Buffalo Bills, Super Bowl XXVIII, Atlanta, Georgia, January 1994

Bruce Davis, Oakland Raiders defeat Washington Redskins, Super Bowl XVIII, Tampa, Florida, January 1987

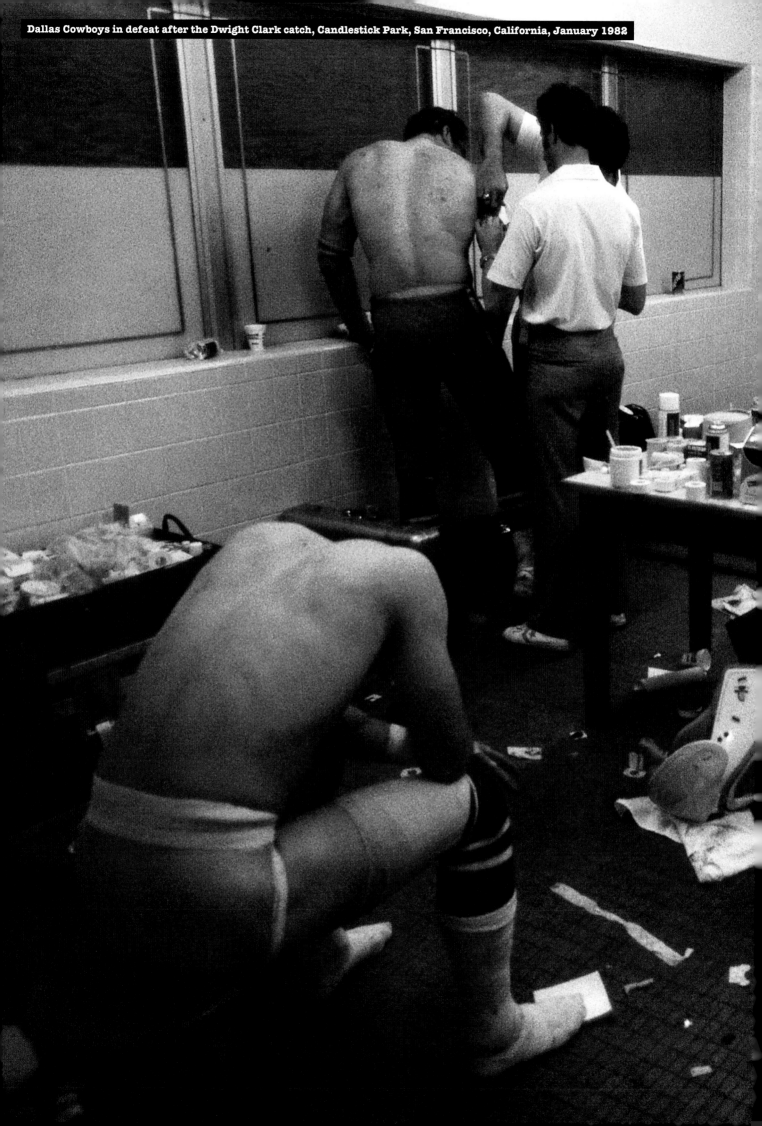

Dallas Cowboys in defeat after the Dwight Clark catch, Candlestick Park, San Francisco, California, January 1982

Dallas Cowboys Player, Halftime, Cleveland, Ohio, December 1980

Bob Brudzinski, Dolphins Training Facility, Miami, Florida, December 1985

Minnesota Vikings vs Tampa Bay Buccaneers, Tampa, Florida, October 1997

Dallas Cowboys, Pontiac Silverdome, Pontiac, Michigan, September 1981

The Orange Bowl, November 1985

Tom Landry, Tex Schramm, Gil Brandt, Clint Murchison, Texas Stadium, Irving, Texas, July 1982

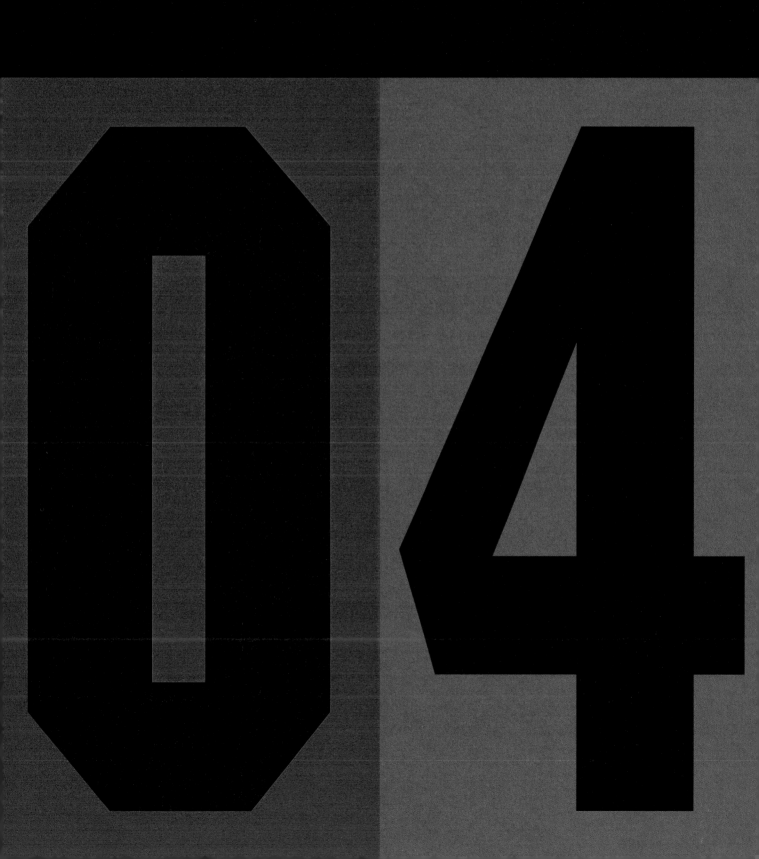

LEGENDS

04

Joe Montana, San Francisco, California, October 1991

John Unitas, Memorial Stadium, Baltimore, Maryland, October 1967

Marcus Allen, Oakland Coliseum, Oakland, California, December 1995

Fran Tarkenton, Minnesota Vikings vs Baltimore Colts, Baltimore, Maryland, October 1967

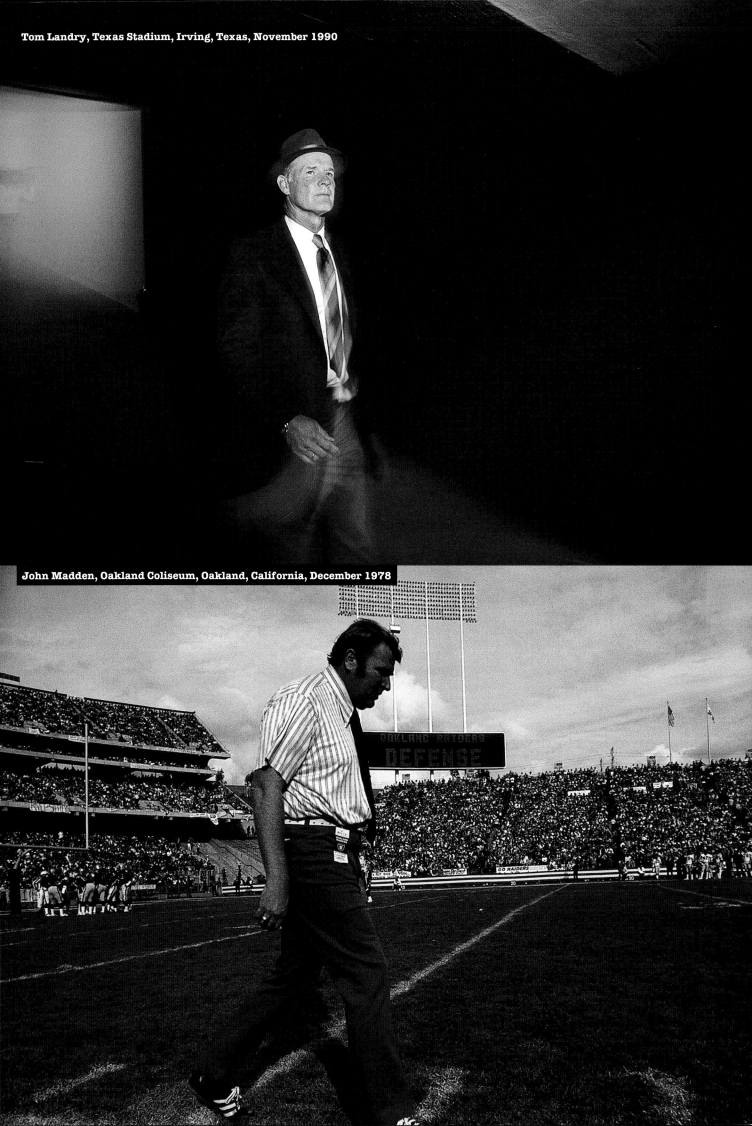

Tom Landry, Texas Stadium, Irving, Texas, November 1990

John Madden, Oakland Coliseum, Oakland, California, December 1978

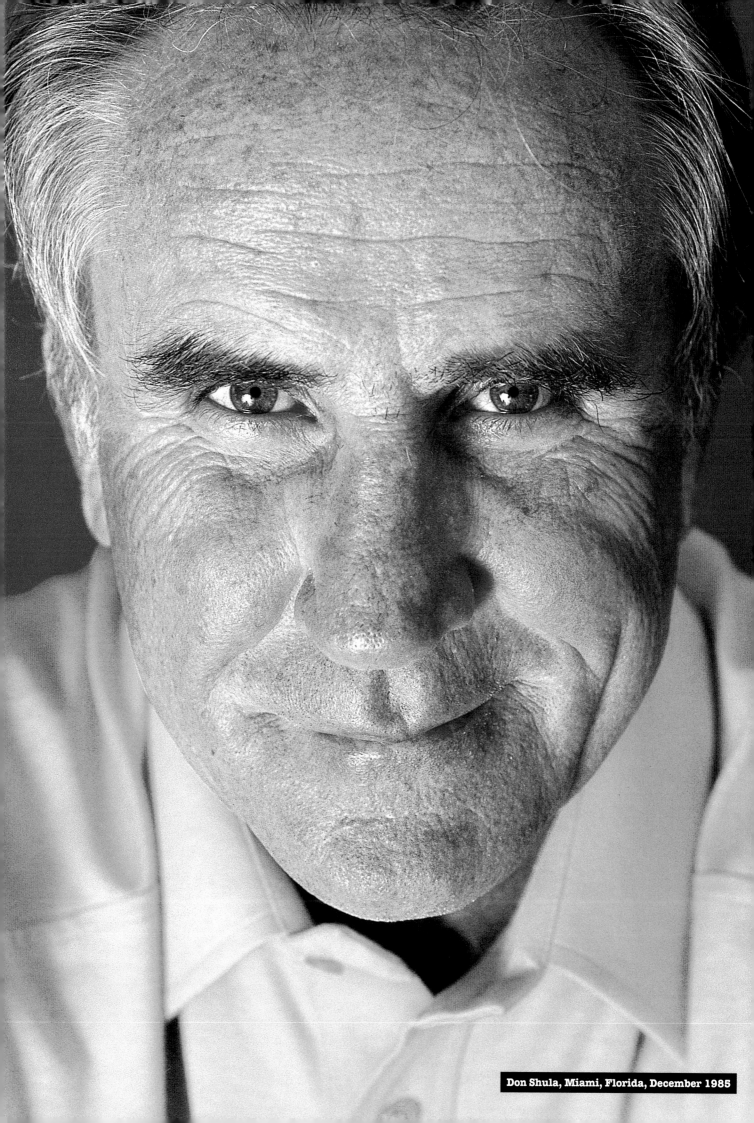

Don Shula, Miami, Florida, December 1985

Vince Lombardi, Memorial Stadium, Baltimore, Maryland, December 1965

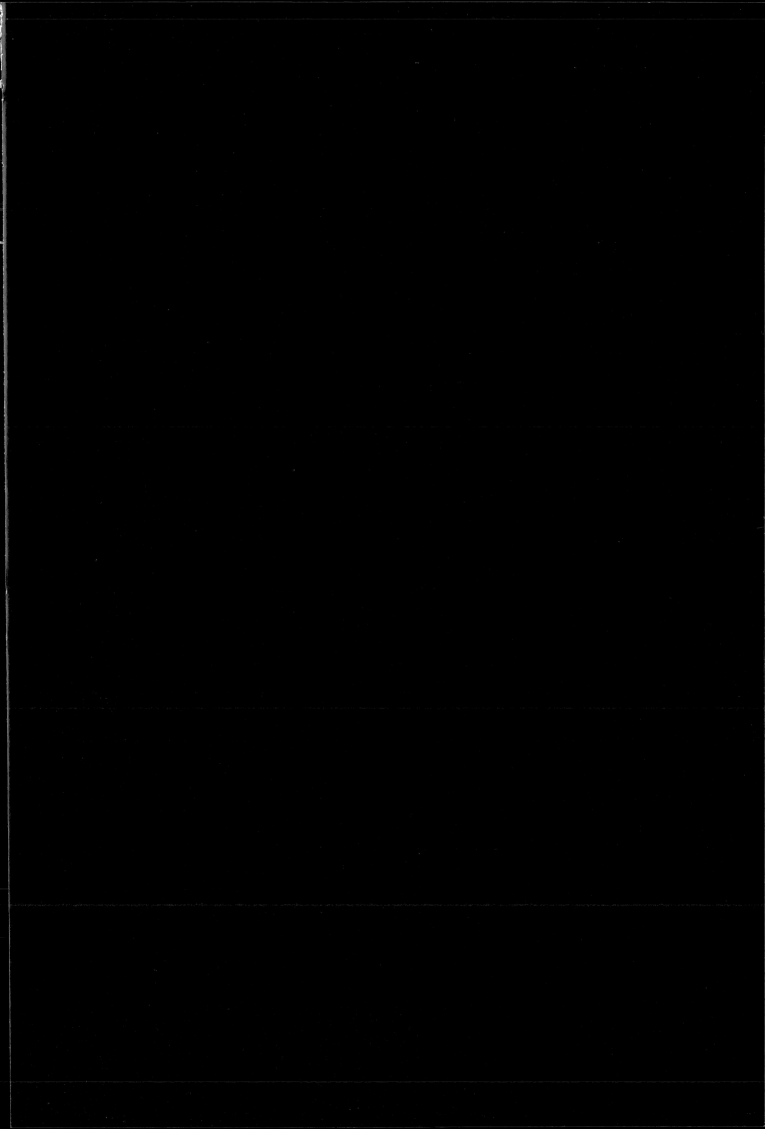

John Unitas, Memorial Stadium, Baltimore, Maryland, December 1970